Sometimes you have to make your own magic.
I have learned that living with depression and surviving with depression are two very different things. My eyes often deceive me.
My heart and my brain are constantly lying to me, but there is some calmness in the act of creation. So I take photos, and I paint, and I write and I occupy my time surrounded by the things and people I love so that I can remind myself that the love is still there. And I have learned that I don't have to be sorry anymore. There is beauty in even the flawed creations that you complete.
That's where the magic is.

CONTENTS

25 Years Buried

It came to me as a dream
a hazy manifestation
Saying, "Follow me. Damnation be blessed"
I accepted my fate
Naye, I fed it
Richness of sweet cherry wine
the luxury of all the finest cuisines
that which I could never afford
Yet still – I had raised this beast
Praised it like the good dog
Insatiable as it was
I became humbled to it's desires
All the while
Noncomplacent to my own

In my mind there is a spiral staircase
Winding upward, endlessly
Into the black hole of my frontal cortex
An elevator would be quicker
Naye, inefficient
Only I have scaled the steps to completion
For the door requires a code of sorts
That I intentionally forget and hide away
None else shall enter
No matter how deserving they may be

It's a parilous flight
Though I am never promised admission
It just happens so many
Convince themselves that they deserve access
Green light?
Naye, red light, high voltage, blaring
Even if I wanted to, I simply couldn't do it
This is where I've hidden away
All the most damned secrets
Events I'd rather forget
It was a parilous flight
Scaling those uneven steps
I dissolve, as a slug in saltwater
Thin air threatening my lungs
Denying me the simple pleasure
Of my own joy

I should expect it by now
Each week I unlock another latch
Uncovering another layer
Of a thing I had long since forgotten
A layer of wallpaper tattered
Plastered over with the newest pattern
A trend to distract my fleeting mind
Though it does seem to give me power
A mirror refracting solar rays
Burns a hole into the weakest spots
Naye, the calculated wax seal
This was my intent
It has always been my intent

And now: I picture myself a harrowing guardian
why I have refused to let you in
To let anyone in to the attic of my thoughts
The horrific things I've seen
Even more horrid implantations I hid
Behind that door, visited hesitantly
Naye, I've lived here
Spent too much time breathing in
The stale dead air
Of decaying matter
Rotting away within those cavities
you would not emerge the same person

I come to assess the wreckage
Knees weak at the exertion
I give into my own head work
I carve the deepest tunnel
Spoonful by spoonful into the cage
Housing my heart
Dump the contents of my forbidden library
Into the housing of that beast
Manifesting a semblance of peace
I presume would occur if only
I'd open the gates

The Forest is Calm

I am a koi, sunshine ricochet off my back
I am swimming downstream
my ambition following close behind
I've threaded unholy water
lost my way and found myself
Far from home

Traveling somewhere
Even I don't know
The current below, leading me on
As evening light takes over
Creates a sparkly film
Over the waters surface

Lilypads dancing about
The promise of longevity here
I lock eyes with a frog
purchased upon a new bloom
as he shoots me a look of warning

The night begins to settle
The moon calling on the nocturne
to bring new life into the waters
From stream to puddle to droplet
Taking final form in the eye of a fox
We have connected
I am aware but I remain unafraid

A single pink leaf lands before me
Enchanting the space I occupy
in abundant wonder
Cherry blossoms rain down
Painting the world as Monet might envision

The fox, in its awe and disbelief
Bows before me, taking in
Each peaceful second of this phenomenon
I turn around, glorious flow of my tail a silken ribbon
Swimming now upstream as I recall
the caution of the frog

The fox, completely engulfed in the pinks and reds
Almost hypnotized by it's beauty
Leaps across the stream
Finding comfort in the nook of a sycamore trunk
It invites me to return home
Allowing me passage, it lays down a paw
now an empty vessel, the fox unveils it's burden

Revealing a family of tree frogs,
Just like the one before
Seven in total, each of them grateful
For a second chance
They leap in unison from lilypad to marshy plain
freedom is granted, a right not a privilege

Fox buries a spent face into clusters
Of fallen pink blossoms, painting the woods
I watch on as the moon grows dim
Swimming into the lowlight

Woman is God

Woman is God
You can't tell me otherwise
Woman is elegantly flowing
Outwardly gathered but
Internally screaming

As she walks half mile
Back and forth and up and down
25 pound bundle of slumber
Attached to her aching chest
Lulling and soothing as
Only a mother could

Woman is God
She is patiently waiting her turn
To simply wedge one word
Into the damnation
She did not order

Just to speak sense into the
Nonsensical, illogical outbursts
Liberally provided by man and child
To be met with "
you should have said so"
Friend... She tried. She did try to
say anything

Woman is God
She is chasing some profound imagery
That tells her some bodies are good
And some of them are not
That her nipples are sacred
But his are free

That she can't hold her face in such a way
Or feel her feelings too boldly
Too fiercely

She must be God
Because man could never
humbly sit in a space
that dictates who and what they are
woman is God
You can't tell me otherwise

Nightwing

The butterfly, beloved
captures everyone's hearts
the image of a meadow
wildflowers Blooming
swarming with a million hues
a billion pollinators
fuzzy yellow bumblers
and yes, the vibrant royal butterfly

How quickly the people of the world
were to label them simply pure
beautiful creatures of solace
the good kind of bug
the kind that doesn't deserve the swatter
you don't kill transformation
change, positivity,luck must persist
the beloved butterfly
good enough to more than just exist

But what of the moth?
the night wings built just the same
alluring patterns, shapes
Present to no other creatures
just as vibrant, just as beautiful
just as striking, yet labeled carelessly
the symbol of death, of misery
The lunar mariposa

Their silken cocoons somehow not enough
their soft velvet wings, insufficient
their feather like antennae
harmless, but feared,destroyed and avoided
sometimes the less appreciated
can be the most extraordinary

Mycophilia

Isn't it curious how the fungus feeds
A mushroom can grow from the death
of some other unfortunately expired soul
Withering away, mossy tuffs fill their shape
whose rotted decaying body created such
nutrients that it brings life to another

If you think about it, one way or another
Dont we all just become the mushroom that feeds
Beckoning for our spirit to take shape
Awakened, no surviving, though surrounded by death
Clutching onto the dust of our bones and such
Latching onto the body that held the soul

A precious life I'm sure, full of soul
one whose heart was once tied to another
Whose body once held defined curves and shape
Or perhaps they were the hand that feeds
Do you think they were ready for death
When the lights dimmed to such...

silence, stillness, emptiness, to such....
Release? Such transience to free the soul!
I wonder if a moment of completion is born in death
If the dance of life and death becoming one another
Sing a melody as the saprophyte feeds
Into tenderized muscle, taking on its shape

The mycelium conjuring up this shape
Filling crevasses that beg questions of the soul
Does the beauty of growth encouraged by death
cycling through one cariosity to another to another
Feeding life offer the bittersweet satisfaction of such
That more than just my curiosity, it feeds?

Little by little the rotting flesh feeds
its not all in vain, dying I mean, just think how such
Exuberance is maintained by the body's recycled soul
Fertilization wholesomely replenishing shape
bringing in light, and love, and completion to another ...
But I do hate to encourage an untimely death

Every soul destined to face their final death
Such a clever cycle,dispersing the energy of another
Taking on the wonderous shape of the fungus
that feeds

Dysmorphia

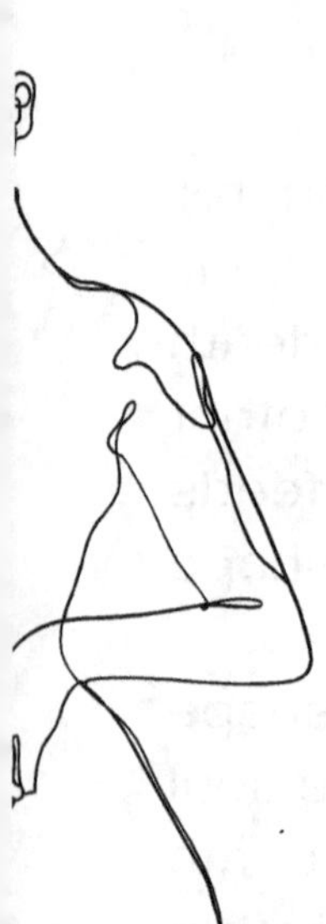

I was dragged
My own body betrayed me - Traitor
Pulling me apart muscle and bone
Brain to one side, skull to the other
Limbs gelatinized
Supporting no bearing
Eyes swollen, pulsating under the pressure
The world shaking within my peripheral
Breathe...
Count to three
Breathe...
Blow out the candles
Heart chugging along the unstable pattern
I think I can I think I can I ...
Can't . . .
Even regulate my temp
It's 56 degrees and my hands are numb
It's 73 degrees I can't feel my toes
Do you hear the ocean? No seashells
What is happening to by body?
The world keeps spinning
My world keeps spinning
I fed you
Nurtured you, did everything right
I bathed you,
Stretched you, exercised your mind

And still you betray me

Worthy

This skin has been so restricted
I'm slowly crawling out of it
Covered in this itchy mesh
That has been holding me captive
For so long
I've simply been dying to get out
Head first I'm plunging
Bursting from layers of eggshell
New
Here I am now

Hello I am refreshed
Hello I am putting myself out there
Vulnerably

Trying something brand new
Expanding the borders
Of my shallow comfort zone
Here I am now
Convincing myself
I too am worthy
That I am talented
That I am good enough
To be seen
And heard
And loved
And just to be

Bathtime

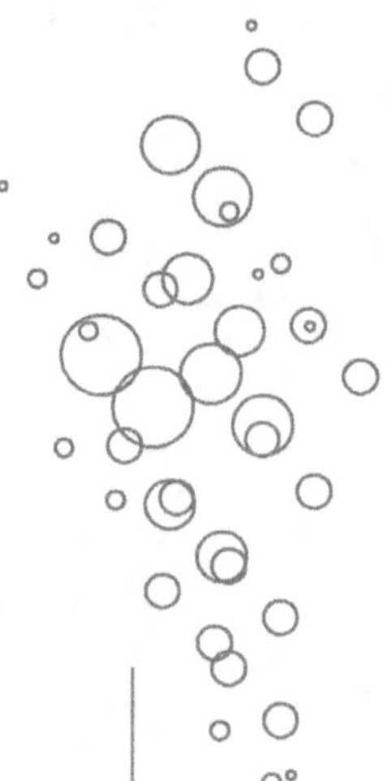

I'm reminded why I don't take baths anymore

whose body is this?
Bouyantly floating curve over curve

I don't know this roundness
belly poking just above the surface
breast hung sloppily on either side
forced to see all these
tiger stripes
they say, they're not so bad

but the folds and creases and looseness
this body that I never pictured
feels foreign to me

Thighs meeting to say hello
as if there were another option
I douse the bubbles over my worst parts
Out of sight out of mind

The shape of a stranger I refuse to see
My otter tattoo swimming happily below
an addition meant to hide the cellulite

They don't remember my yester-body

The three year old carbon copy of myself
comes in to check the temperature
for the twentieth time
pleading to join me
another reminder of who this body belongs to

And where it came from

sometimes bravery comes in the form of protection

I celebrate it in it's many forms
for her sake...
Soon as I close the doors I retaliate
the audacity I must have to punish myself
in my solitude and love myself in company
a lie I hope she never sees through

She says to me, mama has a soft belly like me
mamas milks are nice and full
the sweet ways she points out every flaw

Every piece that I hate the most
The pride she takes in her own body

I hope every time she lays in the bath
ten years from now,
twenty ,
thirty and so
o.n and on eternally

she marvels the beauty and strength that
her body has carried her through
Fuller than before, loose skin or tight
thicker or thinner, she sees every mark, every curve
every last part of herself and she says

my body is a work of art

Just like my Mama's
and that it's not a lie she tells her daughter

Sussarus

Radio silence
Deafeningly quiet
In the cave of my mind
Nothing but the
Drip
     Drip
          Drip
Of my melting thoughts

Oozing through the cracks
Calcium deficient stalagmites
Wrapping tightly through my skull
Suffocating me from
The birdcage of my chest
To the swinging veins
Connecting the heart ...

To the brain
        Through the blood
                Tissue and muscle
To the circuit
Meant to connect
somehow... Disconnected

But the path has been flooded
The electricity seized
Slowly fading out

The deepest breath can't
Quell
Quell
Quell

Reaching for connections
That no longer conduct
A prisoner in a glass box
Sweaty hands longing to catch a grip
Longing ...
...Still
Radio silent
All for the sussarus
Of the Feigning Heart
Saying let it be
And let it go

Stopwatch

I am on borrowed time
In a temporary vehicle
Housing my organs
That are on a lease
When I expire I'll pass them along
Sink my skin and bones into the soil
Lovely fertilizer flourishing the Heathers
Sprouting from between my ribs
And through my empty skull
My soul rising to the occasion
Onto the next
Inhibiting another vehicle
Another home
Another set of organs on lease
On borrowed temporary time

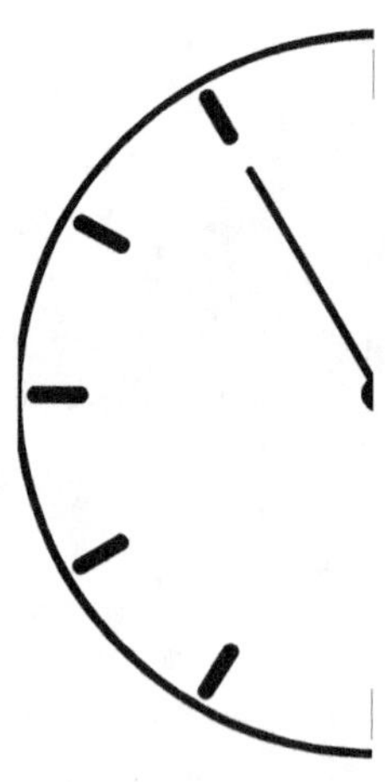

Hand Mirror

Rust speckled glass
Of the brass hand mirror
A reminder
That not everything
That is beautiful
Is perfect
Freckles lining cheekbones
Crooked little teeth
Flushed derma from
Summer to summer
Scarred line after line
After line
And still just as beautiful
Just as precious as the day
Life breathed you in
Kissed your forehead and
Sent you on the way
Clean your lenses off
And peer not beyond the rust
But through it
Even the brassy bits
Are lovely

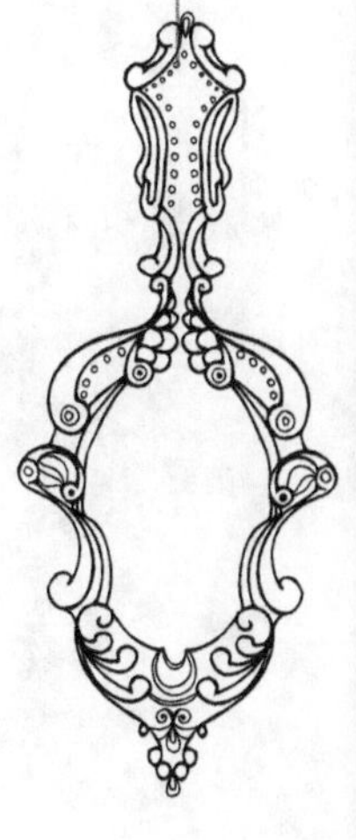

More than Stardust

Who can say
What we are truly
Made of?
We come from the bones
from the blood and spirit
of our fallen ancestors
Our bodies
Built strong and steady
Rising up from the Grit
From rich ashen Earth
Laying foundation for
Great sycamore trees
To touch root
Connecting one life to another
To another to another
Crocheting the pattern
Of simply living
Existing in bodies
That we did not choose
But we learn to
Love their histories
Their structures
To honor their evolutions

We know the formula
The molecular levels
Of our existence

But we must hold purpose
We must be more than stardust

Enough

Sometimes it's just
Not enough

I need to dig my toes
into fresh pillows of Earth
soft and damp, clutching to my skin
Filling my pores delightfully

Feel the rain weigh
My curls into a thick blanket
Across my shoulders
Creating sticky webs
Crawling slyly down my back

Listen to the whistle of the wind
Greeting the leaves with
Its carefully tuned ocarina
Willing even the most mundane
To feel the rhythm

joyously leading the dance
Until every wavering,
breathing,
knowing thing

Every swimming,
swaying,
soul shifting thing
Works together, systematically
creating a machine

Pinch me awake
So it can open my eyes one more time
Awaken my mind that
sometimes,

all of this
is just enough

Drop Off Line

The smell of weed
Ripe and present
7:45 is far too early
All the parents speeding through
Is everyone around here late?
Moms, like zombies herding cattle
Shuffle through the parking lot
As their four year old competes
For Slowest Footsteps
Frustration fuels the morning
A door slams, clunkin' old faithful
The 19-90-something 'vette
It was undoubtedly sharp in its prime
Long since passed
Today, the backseat is covered
In Bluey stickers, and partially eaten breakfast
A mom screams into the void
Sick of the commitment of an
Accidental DIY
Whom she assumes won't notice the regret
carried so heavy on her back each day
Should have used a condom 4 years ago

... But I digress

Your assumptions are wrong
The kids know by the way
They can smell the regret on you
When you walk them to the door
Cursing under your breath
Mad at the world
The consequences of your own actions
You plead with them to just let go
And leave the teary eyed little you
In someone else's hands

At pick up later, you'll have almost forgotten
The chaos of the morning
The way they had you ripping out hair
At 8 a.m. no less
Wide eyed doe gallops towards you
Arms spread open
Wide as the sea
I missed you
I love you
I missed you so much

And Mama look what I drawed for you

Chores

I'm sifting through memories
Of when we were young
When life was supposed to be easy
...
But the laundry never got done

The times when we told ourselves
The best was still in waiting
Withered away silently with every mistake

But the laundry never got done
and the bed was never made
We'd talk our way out of everything
Hoping for better days

We were fixated on trusting each other
Fully and openly
We were conceptualizing
How to never feel lonely
...
But the laundry never got done
And the bed was never made

We were overwhelmed by the mountain of
Dishes that needed to be bathed

There was life to be lived
Experiences to withstand
we'd been cooped up forever

Longing for the time we never knew we had

But the laundry is still not done
And we're not getting younger

Fuck making the bed
We've got joy to discover

The dishes can wait
Theyll be clean when we're dead

We're busy fantasizing
And living outside our heads

I want our kids to say
They enjoyed their childhood
That they're glad we were their parents
They enjoyed every chapter of that book

I want them to feel as if
They were never indisposed
No adult worries or strife to behold

No wasting away, and no missing out
Because that's not what life should be about

We'll do it together
All of it, all at once
so they'll never have to question

...

Is the laundry getting done?

www.ingramcontent.com/pod-product-compliance
Lightning Source LLC
Chambersburg PA
CBHW060925130726
48001CB00006B/2417